COUNTRY PROFILES

ECUADOR

BY GOLRIZ GOLKAR

BELLWETHER MEDIA • MINNEAPOLIS, MN

Blastoff! Discovery launches a new mission: reading to learn. Filled with facts and features, each book offers you an exciting new world to explore!

BLASTOFF! UNIVERSE

BLASTOFF! Beginners — GRADE K

BLASTOFF! READERS — GRADES 1-3

DISCOVERY — GRADE 4

This edition first published in 2022 by Bellwether Media, Inc.

No part of this publication may be reproduced in whole or in part without written permission of the publisher.
For information regarding permission, write to Bellwether Media, Inc.,
Attention: Permissions Department,
6012 Blue Circle Drive, Minnetonka, MN 55343.

Library of Congress Cataloging-in-Publication Data

Names: Golkar, Golriz, author.
Title: Ecuador / by Golriz Golkar.
Description: Minneapolis, MN : Bellwether Media, [2022] |
    Series: Country profile | Includes bibliographical references and
    index. | Audience: Ages 7-13 | Audience: Grades 4-6 | Summary:
    "Engaging images accompany information about Ecuador. The
    combination of high-interest subject matter and narrative text is
    intended for students in grades 3 through 8." Provided by publisher.
Identifiers: LCCN 2021051731 (print) | LCCN 2021051732 (ebook)
    | ISBN 9781644876107 (library binding) |
    ISBN 9781648346217 (ebook)
Subjects: LCSH: Ecuador–Juvenile literature.
Classification: LCC F3708.5 .G65 2022 (print) |
    LCC F3708.5 (ebook) | DDC 986.6–dc23/eng/20211026
LC record available at https://lccn.loc.gov/2021051731
LC ebook record available at https://lccn.loc.gov/2021051732

Editor: Rachael Barnes   Designer: Brittany McIntosh

Printed in the United States of America, North Mankato, MN.

TABLE OF CONTENTS

LAS PEÑAS
GUAYAQUIL

A family climbs a long stone staircase in the Las Peñas district of Guayaquil. From the top, they pause to watch the gleaming Guayas River below. They walk by the multicolored houses of the city's oldest neighborhood. Some of the homes are now small cafés. Stopping in one for lunch, the family enjoys fresh *encocado*, or fish with coconut sauce.

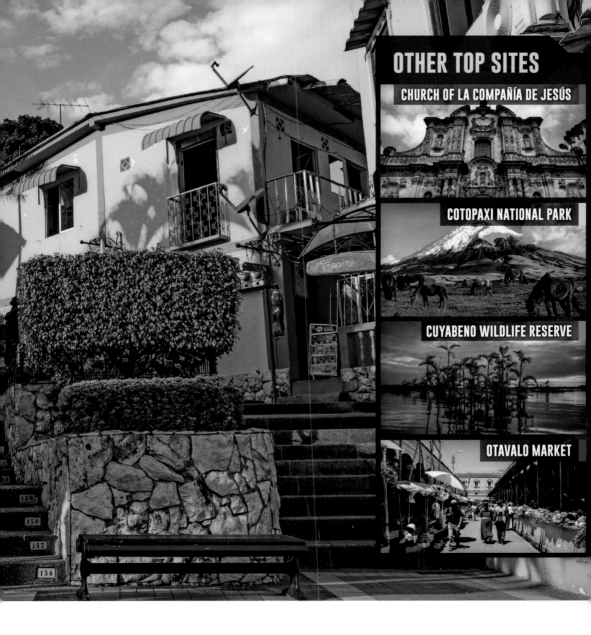

OTHER TOP SITES

CHURCH OF LA COMPAÑÍA DE JESÚS

COTOPAXI NATIONAL PARK

CUYABENO WILDLIFE RESERVE

OTAVALO MARKET

In the afternoon, they stroll along the boardwalk. They enjoy the historic buildings, such as the Torre Morisca clock tower. After, they shop for handmade **souvenirs** at the Mercado Artesanal. **Culture** and delicious food are just some of the wonders of Ecuador!

COLOMBIA

Ecuador is located in northwestern South America. It covers 109,484 square miles (283,561 square kilometers). The country is located on the **equator**. It borders the Pacific Ocean to the west. Colombia lies to the north. Peru surrounds Ecuador to the east and the south.

Quito, the capital, is located in the Andean highlands in north-central Ecuador. Puná Island sits off the southern coast. It lies in the **Gulf** of Guayaquil. The **volcanic** Galápagos Islands are west of the **mainland** in the Pacific Ocean. They consist of 19 islands and many **islets**.

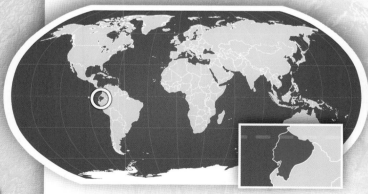

PERU

LANDSCAPE AND CLIMATE

Ecuador's mainland switches between mountains and valleys. Sandy beaches and low mountain ranges line the coast. Rich lowlands stretch across the country's western region into central Ecuador. The volcanic Andes Mountains stand tall in the central highland region. To the east, lowlands become part of the Amazon **Rain Forest**.

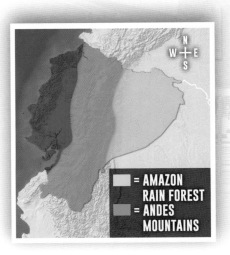

= AMAZON RAIN FOREST
= ANDES MOUNTAINS

HOW HIGH CAN YOU GO?

Mount Chimborazo is Ecuador's tallest mountain. It is also the point on Earth closest to outer space!

AMAZON
RAIN FOREST

QUITO

Average seasonal highs and lows

JANUARY
HIGH: 67 °F (19 °C)
LOW: 50 °F (10 °C)

APRIL
HIGH: 66 °F (19 °C)
LOW: 50 °F (10 °C)

JULY
HIGH: 68 °F (20 °C)
LOW: 49 °F (9 °C)

OCTOBER
HIGH: 68 °F (20 °C)
LOW: 49 °F (9 °C)

°F = degrees Fahrenheit
°C = degrees Celsius

Much of Ecuador has a **tropical** climate. The lowlands and central valleys are hot and sticky. Mountaintops can be cold and snowy. In coastal areas, the ocean affects the temperature. Ecuador has two seasons. The wet season is generally between October and May. June to September is the dry season in many regions.

KINKAJOU

Ecuador's different regions are home to many animals. Jaguars and ocelots roam the rain forest. They hunt birds, fish, and rodents. Howler monkeys let out a low-pitched call as they climb through the trees. Raccoon-like kinkajous scurry about at night. Foxes, pumas, and tapirs roam the mountains. The Andean condor, the national animal, circles above.

ANDEAN CONDOR

Marine and land iguanas sunbathe on the Galápagos Islands. Galápagos giant tortoises rest in mud puddles when they are not munching on cactuses. Blue-footed boobies and Galápagos penguins waddle about. These birds feast on small fish, such as sardines. Hammerhead sharks and spotted-eagle rays swim nearby.

MARINE IGUANA

GALÁPAGOS GIANT TORTOISE

EXPLORING THE GALÁPAGOS ISLANDS

In 1835, scientist Charles Darwin visited the Galápagos Islands. He studied the wildlife on the islands. His work led to his book, *On the Origin of Species*, and the theory of evolution.

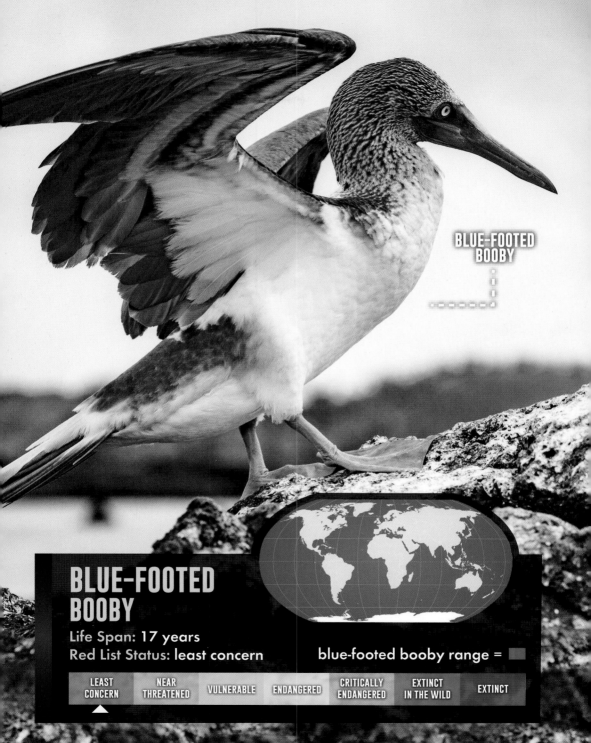

BLUE-FOOTED
BOOBY

BLUE-FOOTED
BOOBY
Life Span: 17 years
Red List Status: least concern

blue-footed booby range =

LEAST CONCERN	NEAR THREATENED	VULNERABLE	ENDANGERED	CRITICALLY ENDANGERED	EXTINCT IN THE WILD	EXTINCT

More than 17 million people live in Ecuador. Around 7 out of every 10 Ecuadorians are *mestizo*. They have mixed **native** and European roots. Other Ecuadorians are native to the country. Some residents have African **ancestry**.

Most Ecuadorians are Roman Catholic. A small number are Evangelical Christians. Spanish is the official language of Ecuador. Native groups in the highland region speak Kichwa and Shuar. In other regions, native groups speak their own languages.

FAMOUS FACE

Name: Jefferson Perez
Birthday: July 1, 1974
Hometown: Cuenca, Ecuador
Famous for: The first-ever Olympic medalist for Ecuador, he holds a gold and a silver medal in race walking

SPEAK SPANISH

ENGLISH	SPANISH	HOW TO SAY IT
hello	hola	OH-lah
goodbye	adiós	ah-dee-OHS
please	por favor	pohr fah-VOR
thank you	gracias	grah-SEE-ahs
yes	sí	SEE
no	no	noh

CUENCA

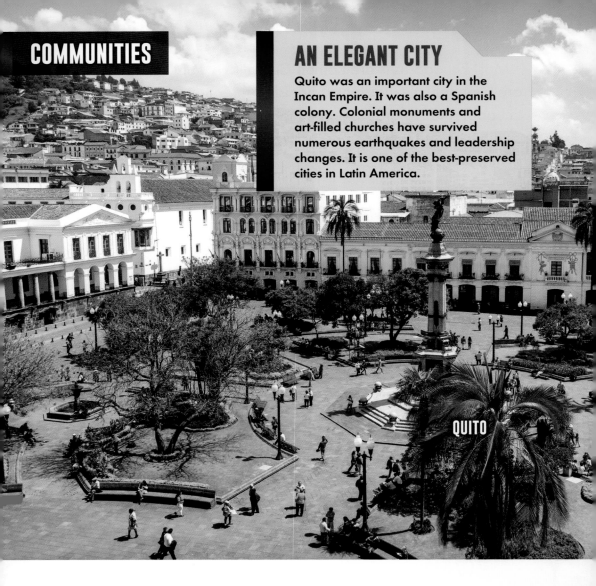

AN ELEGANT CITY

Quito was an important city in the Incan Empire. It was also a Spanish colony. Colonial monuments and art-filled churches have survived numerous earthquakes and leadership changes. It is one of the best-preserved cities in Latin America.

QUITO

Most Ecuadorians live in **urban** areas. In the Andean highlands, Quito and Cuenca are the largest cities. There, people live in Spanish-style apartments or concrete houses. Buses, taxis, and local trains help people get around. Along the coast, many people live in or around Guayaquil. Some people live in simple apartments or small houses on stilts. Buses are commonly used there.

People in **rural** areas of the eastern lowlands live in palm leaf houses. They often live in small villages. Canoes carry people in roadless jungle areas.

Ecuadorian families are close. Many generations may live together. Grandparents often help raise their grandchildren.

Ecuadorians are warm and polite. They greet strangers with a handshake. Strangers are addressed by title and last name. Women often meet with a kiss on the cheek. Only friends and family address each other by their first names.

MARIMBA
PERFORMANCE

Ecuadorians love music. *Marimba* is especially enjoyed on the northern coast. Ecuadorians dance to a wood xylophone and drums. *Bomba* is popular in the Andean highlands. It mixes African beats with the Andean guitar. Women may dance while balancing a bottle on their heads. *Pasillo* is the national music. Slow songs are sung to gentle guitar music.

Ecuadorian children receive free public education. They must attend school from ages 6 to 14. After high school, students who pass a test may attend university or job training programs.

About one in four Ecuadorians works in agriculture. Many rural Ecuadorians grow crops, such as corn, potatoes, and beans. Others work on large banana or cacao **plantations**. Some Ecuadorians work on oil drilling sites. Many Ecuadorians own small businesses. Others have office jobs or work in the **tourism** industry.

BANANA PLANTATION

PANAMA HATS... FROM ECUADOR!

The popular handwoven Panama hat is actually made in Ecuador. The hats are woven from toquilla palm leaves and take months to make.

SOCCER

Soccer is a favorite sport in Ecuador. The Ecuadorian national team has played in **World Cup** games. Volleyball and basketball are also popular. Ecuadorians keep **tradition** alive by playing *pelota nacional*. This sport is played with a small, heavy ball and wooden rackets. It is commonly played by men in the northern Andean region on Sundays.

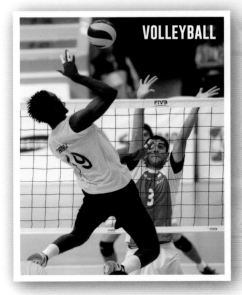

VOLLEYBALL

Ecuadorians enjoy many outdoor activities. Cycling is popular. In Quito, large streets are closed to traffic on Sundays and open to bicycles. Ecuadorians also relax by visiting beaches and bathing in natural **hot springs**. Children play outdoor games like hopscotch, hide-and-seek, and ball games.

HOT SPRINGS

EL QUEMADO (THE BURNED)

What You Need:
- two even teams with at least two players each
- one large soft ball (like a dodgeball)
- a cone or rope to divide the field into two sides

How to Play:
1. Make two teams with an equal number of players.
2. Each team stands on opposite sides of the playing field. Choose one team to start.
3. A player from the starting team throws the ball at the other team's players. The goal is to "burn" those players by touching them with the ball.
4. If a player is touched, they are out, or "burned." If the ball is caught, the player who caught it stays in the game.
5. Any player who catches the ball can throw it at the other team. If no one catches the ball, a player on the ball's side of the field can pick it up and throw it at the other team.
6. The teams keep throwing the ball at each other until an entire team is out. The last team standing wins!

MMMM... CHOCOLATE!

Ecuador is one of the world's biggest producers of cacao beans. Cacao Arriba beans are used to make fine chocolate. Many people believe Ecuadorian cacao is the best in the world!

TOASTING CACAO BEANS

Ecuadorian meals are rich and tasty. Chicken and pork are favorites in many regions. Coastal Ecuadorians eat more fish. Meals often include corn and potatoes or rice and beans as sides. Soup and fresh fruits are eaten throughout Ecuador.

An Ecuadorian breakfast includes coffee, potatoes or rice, and eggs or fruit. Lunch is the main meal. A typical lunch dish is seafood *ceviche*, prepared with lime and onions. *Seco de pollo* is a popular spicy chicken stew. *Cuy*, or roasted guinea pig, is an Andean favorite. For a snack, people eat street foods like *empanadas de viento*. These pastries are filled with cheese and onions.

CEVICHE

CUY

EMPANADAS DE VIENTO

ESPUMILLAS (GUAVA MERINGUE CREAM)

Espumillas are a popular dessert eaten at home or bought from street carts. Ask an adult to help with this recipe.

Ingredients:
8 cups of very ripe guavas
2 cups sugar, divided
1/3 cup water
2 egg whites
Colorful sprinkles and berry syrup for topping
Optional: ice cream cones

Steps:
1. Peel the guavas with a vegetable peeler to remove the skin. Then, remove the seeds.

2. Using a fork, mash the guava in a large bowl and blend it with 1 cup of sugar.

3. Heat water and 1 cup of sugar on the stove to about 240 degrees Fahrenheit (116 degrees Celsius) to make syrup.

4. Beat the egg whites with an electric mixer. Slowly add in the fruit mixture until everything is creamy and stiff.

5. With the electric mixer going, slowly pour in the hot syrup. Mix until stiff peaks form.

6. Serve in ice cream cones or bowls. Add berry syrup and sprinkles as toppings.

CARNAVAL

Ecuadorians celebrate many holidays. On New Year's Eve, families create paper **effigies** called *monigote*. They represent the old year and are placed in front of each home. At midnight, families burn them to bring a fresh start to the new year. *Carnaval* is a religious celebration in February. Ecuadorians enjoy parades, dances, and foam and water fights for several days.

In June, native groups celebrate *Inti Raymi*, the Festival of the Sun. They thank nature through music and dance. Independence Day is celebrated on August 10. Communities enjoy music, military parades, and feasts. Ecuadorians are proud to celebrate their lively country!

INTI RAYMI

1450s
Incas of Peru conquer the Caras people, whose kingdom is based in Quito

1822
Antonio José de Sucre defeats the Spanish to make Ecuador part of independent Gran Colombia

1534
Spanish troops conquer Ecuador and make the country part of the Spanish Viceroyalty of Peru

1830
Ecuador leaves Gran Colombia and becomes an independent republic

1998

Ecuador signs an agreement with Peru to gain land and river navigation rights

1941

Peru begins a decades-long conflict with Ecuador over unsettled, mineral-rich Amazon territory

2021

Neisi Dajomes Barrera is Ecuador's first female Olympic gold medalist after winning the 76 kilogram weightlifting event

2007

President Rafael Correa begins a strict 10-year rule over Ecuador

1948

Galo Plaza Lasso begins what will become the first full term of a freely elected president since the country became a republic

ECUADOR FACTS

Official Name: Republic of Ecuador

Flag of Ecuador: The Ecuadorian flag has three horizontal bands. The top, double-width band of yellow represents rich natural resources. The middle blue band represents the sky, sea, and rivers. The bottom red band represents blood spilled during the wars fought for freedom. On the center of the flag is Ecuador's coat of arms. Among the details are images of the national bird, the Guayas River, and Mount Chimborazo as symbols of the country's beauty, wealth, and strength.

Area: 109,484 square miles
(283,561 square kilometers)

Capital City: Quito

Important Cities: Cuenca, Guayaquil, Santo Domingo

Population:
17,093,159 (July 2021)

WHERE PEOPLE LIVE

COUNTRYSIDE
35.6%

CITY
64.4%